Dear Mom & Dad,

    I just thought that you would like this book to see what I saw this summer in Canada.

Love
Andy

W9-AZC-000

Dear Mom & Dad,

I just thought that you would like this book to see what I saw this summer in Canada.

W9-AZC-000

THE CANADIAN
ROCKIES

KARA KURYLLOWICZ

Published and Distributed by:

Irving Weisdorf & Co. Ltd.

International Publishers and Distributors

2801 John Street
Markham, Ontario, Canada
L3R 2Y8

(905)477-9901

Writer
Kara Kuryllowicz

Editor
Susan Gerard

Book Design
David Villavera

Artist
Michael Graf

Typography
Nancy MacKay

ISBN: 0-921978-89-8

P H O T O G R A P H Y

ANIMALS ANIMALS/ EARTH SCENES

Johnny Johnson
24

BIRDS EYE VIEW PHOTO

Ron Garnett
14, 19, 48, 80, 94, 99, 103

Derek Bodington
101

CP ARCHIVES
33

FIRST LIGHT

Thomas Kitchin
22

Patrick Morrow
39

Robert Lankinen
88

Larry Fisher
8, 9, 11, 12, 17, 20/21, 32, 49, 60/61,
62, 63, 71, 92, 95, 97, Back cover

Terry Parker
16, 47, 53, 58, 73, 100

THE IMAGE BANK

Grant V. Faint
23, 43

Harald Sund
70

Eddie Hironaka
81

VIEWPOINTS WEST

Murray O'Neill
26, 40, 57

Paul Morrison
51, 34/35, 105

Kaj Svensson
75

MASTERFILE

Daryl Benson
29, 36, 42, 56, 76, 77, 79,
85, 102, 106

Garry Black
107

Hans Blohm
109

Bill Brooks
44, 45, 52, 54, 55, 59, 67,
90, 108

Gloria Chomica
28, 72

Miles Ertman
Front cover, 98

Tim Fitzharris
3, 65, 66, 82/83

John Foster
30

Ted Grant
110/111

Sherman Hines
25, 78

J.A. Kraulis
27, 41, 46, 50, 68/69, 89, 91

Wayne Lynch
18

Barrett & MacKay
15

Alec Pytlowany
93

Wilhelm Schmidt
31, 84

Greg Stott
87

Mark Tomalty
4/5, 112

John de Visser
37

Douglas E. Walker
74

Contents

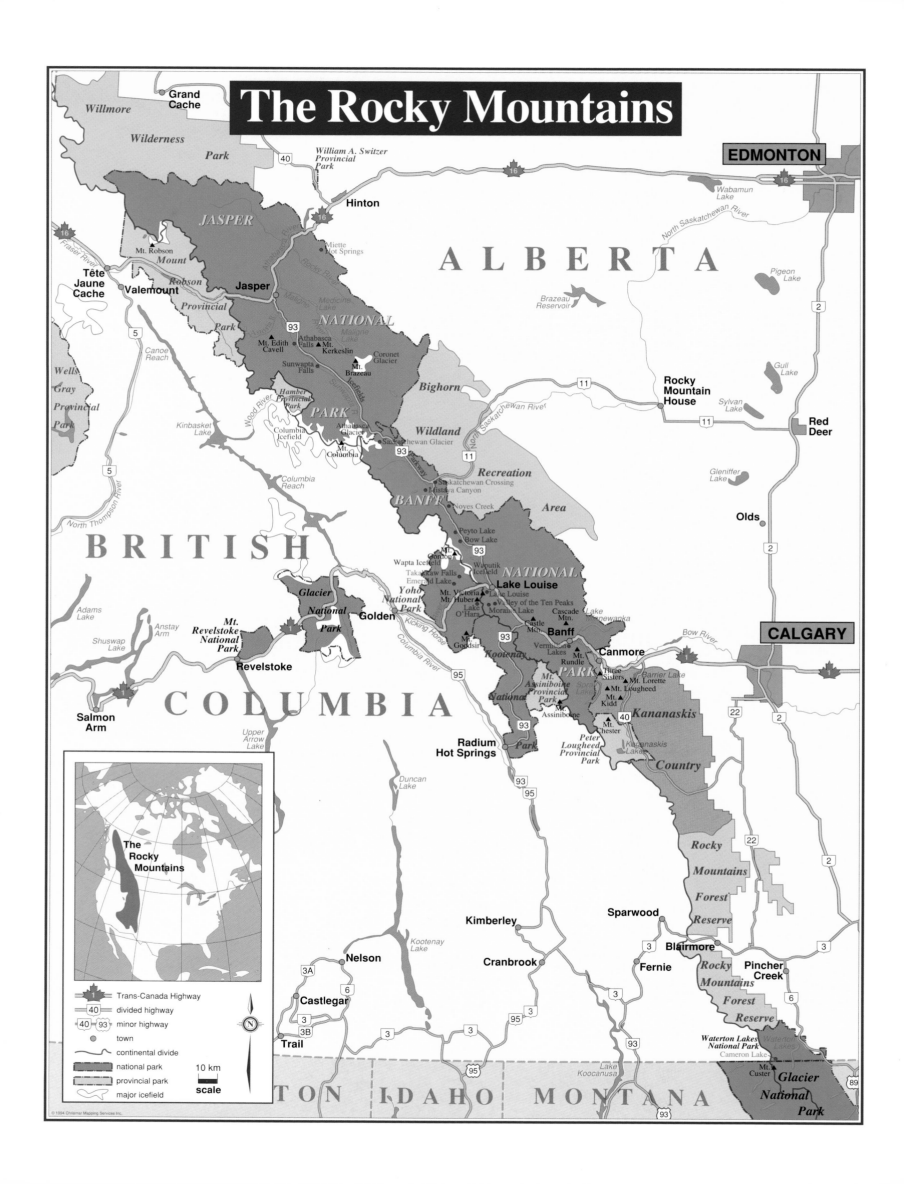

The Rocky Mountains

EDMONTON

CALGARY

A L B E R T A

B R I T I S H

C O L U M B I A

IDAHO   MONTANA

Legend:
- ⬥ Trans-Canada Highway
- 40 divided highway
- 40 / 93 minor highway
- ● town
- continental divide
- national park
- provincial park
- major icefield
- 10 km scale

N

© 1994 Chinamar Mapping Services Inc.

THE CANADIAN ROCKIES

Wild, rugged and proud, the Rockies are at their most spectacular in Canada, although the ranges run from the most northerly Yukon Territories, all the way south to Mexico.

The Rockies follow the great Continental Divide, along the Alberta/British Columbia border, framed to the east by never-ending prairie plains and to the west by the rich, deep valley of the Rocky Mountain Trench.

The alpine landscapes of the Canadian Rockies have been recognized worldwide for more than a century. In 1752, Leguardeur St. Pierre christened these mountains "Montagnes de Roches" or Mountains of Rock. But, the Stoney Natives, who called these ranges their own for 100,000 years, knew them as the "Shining Mountains", which says more about these natural wonders than the "Rockies" ever could.

Dominating national parks dotted throughout Alberta and British Columbia, the Rocky Mountains originally served only to awe tourists and service the railway. More recently, they are fittingly revered as wilderness preserves dedicated to nature and her children.

Today, the Canadian Rockies are a much needed haven for entire mountain ecosystems, fiercely and loyally protected in one of the world's largest national park groupings.

Banff National Park became Canada's first national park in 1887, two years after the area around the Cave and Basin Hot Springs was marked for development as a park and European-style spa. Three years later, Banff National Park was enlarged to its present size of 6,640 sq. km. (2,564 sq. mi.). Other national parks followed soon after, Yoho (1886), Glacier (1886), Waterton Lakes (1895), Jasper (1907), Mount Revelstoke (1914) and Kootenay (1920).

Only those who "need to reside" in the parks actually live there, for example, employees of the parks and vital services. As all park land is Crown-owned, homeowners, businesses and hotels lease their lands from the Canadian Parks Service and pay annual land taxes.

Since 1984, the United Nations has considered the Banff, Jasper, Yoho and Kootenay National Parks a huge (20,160 sq.km./7,782 sq. mi.) World Heritage Site. In 1990, Mount Assiniboine, Mount Robson and Hamber Provincial Parks were also included.

Known and loved all over the world, Banff, Jasper and Waterton Lakes on the east slope of the Rockies in Alberta and Kootenay and Yoho on the western slopes in British Columbia are the Rocky Mountains' true gems.

There are still pockets of civilization in the parks, havens for mankind, in the form of towns and villages, with a myriad of hotels, restaurants and amenities.

David Thompson was the first European to brave the Rockies to see if the Columbia River could be used to move furs to the coast. By 1811, he'd reached the river's mouth at the Pacific Ocean. By 1845, beaver had grown scarce and demand died down, giving way to the gold rush in the Fraser River and Cariboo valleys.

Thanks to the North-West Mounted Police, the untamed Canadian west was more peaceful and civilized than the legendary Wild West of the United States. They controlled the whiskey trade and signed treaties with local Indian tribes starting in 1875. Now the Royal Canadian Mounted Police, the RCMP or the "Mounties" in their red coats are an internationally recognized symbol of Canada.

The singular peace of distant Rocky Mountain peaks - it seeps beneath the skin and settles quietly next to your soul, whether you're luxuriating in the solitary splendor of a remote area or revelling in the spectacle of the mountains and the Bow River from the Banff Springs Hotel's heated, outdoor pool.

The true magic of the Rocky Mountains is in shafts of sunlight lingering on snow-capped mountains, before moving gently to drop swiftly below the horizon.

Experience for yourself the wonder, the awe and even the affection the Stoney Natives felt for these shining mountains.

Banff National Park

MOUNT RUNDLE
Above

Mount Rundle, a wall of solid limestone soaring above Vermilion Lakes, was layers of silt on the floor of an ancient ocean millions of years ago.

BANFF SPRINGS HOTEL
Left

Towering above the Banff Springs Hotel, Mount Rundle dwarfs the gracious old dowager as she sits, nestled amidst the trees on the valley's floor.

BANFF NATIONAL PARK

Serene lakes, sparkling streams, tumbling waterfalls, narrow gullies, forested valleys, flowered meadows and above it all, the mountains in all their glory.

Amidst an array of natural wonders that ring the town like precious jewels, the hotels and restaurants of Banff are just moments from great wilderness and the option of primitive camping in the rugged outdoors.

When hot springs were discovered near what is now the Banff townsite, everyone wanted the springs for their very own. Of course, visions of potential profits pitted man against man and it became apparent only government intervention would get people to share these natural wonders.

A "hot" property then and now, even the most jaded visitor lets the heat of the springs soothe aching bodies and tired minds. Built around the springs, the resorts brought the railways much needed revenue, ensuring the survival of a young Canada.

The Upper Hot Springs and the Cave and Basin Springs each have a unique character, with individual flow volumes, chemical composition and temperature. The Upper Hot Springs are slightly warmer than the Cave and have a distinctive scent due to the water's high sulphur content. The Cave and Basin springs were a rare and special treat when the wild west was bereft of plumbing back in the late 1800s, but souvenir hunters who should have known better stole the stalactites that graced these time-worn walls piece by piece. We'd like to think today's more environmentally aware tourists would have let them be.

In 1855, a small 26 sq. km. Federal Reserve was created around the springs and by 1930, Banff National Park's size was fixed at 6,641 sq. km. (2,564 sq. mi.). Lord Strathcona, a director of the Canadian Pacific Railway (CPR), christened the area "Banff" after his Scottish birthplace. It's also said the town was named for "Banffshire" the birthplace of the CPR's president George Stephen.

The trail from Banff to Lake Louise and north to Jasper through Roger's Pass to British Columbia was a long and dusty one. By 1921 a proper road connected Banff to Lake Louise and finally in 1940, the road reached Jasper. But it was 1962, before the Trans-Canada Highway reached through Roger's Pass to British Columbia.

To really appreciate the best of Banff a visit to some of the area's most beautiful and fascinating natural attractions is a must. A 4.5 km drive beside Vermilion Lakes gives visitors the opportunity to see some of Canada's most interesting wildlife such as the bald eagle or a bighorn sheep. Or take a brisk stroll through the Bow River and Hoodoos trail. This trail of discovery takes visitors through wildflower-strewn meadows beside the Bow River, up a hillside standing tall with fir and pine trees to Tunnel Mountain and then on to the dramatic, mystical Hoodoos, natural structures the Stoney Natives once believed came alive at night to guard the tunnel.

The Park is protective of nature's treasures and stresses the importance of not disturbing the natural order of things such as not feeding the animals or collecting wildflowers.

Today, Banff attracts those seeking the Rockies' wildest, most remote areas as well as those who'd rather enjoy the mountains in the most luxurious comfort. Banff has your perfect answer.

WINTER WONDERLAND
Above

Snow-dusted, this fairytale landscape boasts a castle of its very own, the magical Banff Springs Hotel. Flakes float gently through dusky skies as night falls on silence.

THE COUGAR
Above

The cougar, puma or mountain lion is so rare in the parks, that seeing one is a special treat. The first park wardens killed "unwanted" wildlife, exterminating over 80 cougars in Banff and Jasper parks between 1924 and 1941.

BANFF AVENUE
Left

Picture-perfect and snug against the base of Cascade Mountain, it's obvious why this classic postcard view of Banff Avenue is such a perfect reminder of this classic resort town.

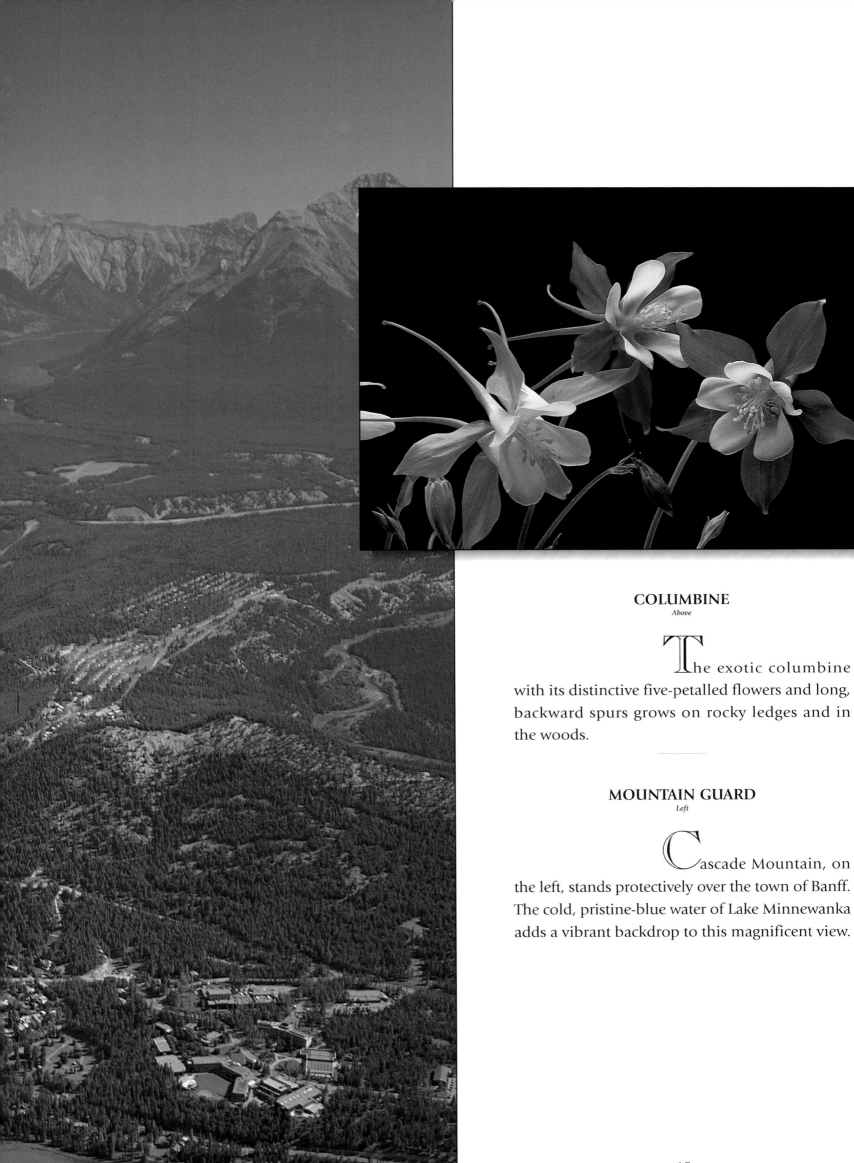

COLUMBINE
Above

The exotic columbine with its distinctive five-petalled flowers and long, backward spurs grows on rocky ledges and in the woods.

MOUNTAIN GUARD
Left

Cascade Mountain, on the left, stands protectively over the town of Banff. The cold, pristine-blue water of Lake Minnewanka adds a vibrant backdrop to this magnificent view.

MOUNTAIN GOAT
Above

Perfectly adapted to the harsh mountain environment, mountain goats have hooves with flexible toes and "no skid" soles for clambering about their alpine homes. To protect the new kid(s) from predators, nannies usually give birth on the ledge of a cliff.

BOW VALLEY
Right

Under moonlit skies, Mount Rundle looms over Bow Valley and the town of Banff. The Valley offers a tranquil home to both human and animal members of the Rocky Mountain population.

ICEFIELDS PARKWAY
Above

Now an internationally recognized cycling route, with just two major passes to climb and awesome scenery around every bend, the north-south Icefields Parkway, is one of just two major roads through the park.

WESTERN BLUEBIRD
Left

Part of the robin family, this dramatically coloured red-breasted western bluebird makes its nest in holes in trees. The male of the species boasts brighter colours than its female counterpart and serenades her with a warbling mating call.

MOOSE
Above

The moose, with its long, lean legs, rounded shoulders and large antlers, is a familiar sight on the valley floor of the Rockies. Preferring its own company to that of a herd, the moose stays close to lush, densely treed areas.

MOUNT ASSINIBOINE
Previous page

Mount Assiniboine appears to lord it over its subjects. When Robert L. Barrett came to Mount Assiniboine in 1893, he agreed that "it was uphill all the way to the top and was not a one boy job."

BALD EAGLE
Above

With its large, hooked bill, sharp, curled talons and powerful wingspan that can measure up to six feet (180cm.) in full flight, the bald eagle is a formidable opponent for the more vulnerable mountain wildlife. Although protected by law, this predator is still a rare, but majestic, sight in the Rockies.

WILDLIFE PARADISE
Right

The Vermilion Lakes, spectacularly lit by the prairie sun, are home to elk, mule deer, coyote and bear and, as the temperature falls, wolves. In the summer, the haunting cry of the loon rings clear and true.

ALPINE LARCH
Above

Evergreen only as long as the summer sun shines, the alpine larch turns to gold come fall, then drops its needles. It grows on the rockiest of soils, even in crevices on steep, rugged slopes and is important because it controls run-off and erosion.

GRIZZLY BEAR
Left

Grizzlies use their long, curved claws (up to six inches) to dig up their favourite foods, roots and tubers. You'll also recognize the grizzly by the distinctive hump over its shoulders and its concave face.

HORNED OWL
Above

The great horned owl is a powerful predator that eats rodents and small birds. It can be up to two feet (60 cm.) long and the females may have a wing span of 200 cm. (80 in.).

INDIAN PAINTBRUSH
Right

Deceivingly beautiful, the Indian paintbrush is a parasitic plant that takes its nourishment from the roots of other plants.

MALLARD DUCK
Above

The male mallard catches the eye. The best known of Canada's ducks, the male of the species is distinguishable by its green-glossed head and elegant body colouring.

CASCADE MOUNTAIN
Right

More interested in shooting big game than capturing the marvelous views, the first tourist to visit the area in 1859-1860 deemed Cascade Mountain "in no way remarkable".

BOW VALLEY
Above

Vibrant hues of silver, blue and emerald - when visionary Canadian Pacific Railway manager William C. Van Horne saw the Bow Valley, he reasoned, "If we can't export the scenery, we'll import the tourists."

BULL ELK
Left

Elk or "wapiti", which means "rear end" in Shawnee, are distinguished by their large straw-coloured rumps and stumpy tails. The elk population mushroomed after predators like the cougar and wolf were "eliminated" and park rangers were "forced" to exterminate them. Today, man is learning to let nature do her own balancing.

Lake Louise

THE VALLEY OF GIANTS
Above

Lake Louise is set like a precious jewel in a valley ringed by Mount Victoria, Fairview Mountain, Mount Lefroy, Mount Whyte and Mount St. Piran.

LAKE LOUISE
Left

The sun rises on Lake Louise and those who are privy to the grandeur and pristine beauty of the Rocky Mountain ranges are truly blessed.

LAKE LOUISE REGION

Still part of Banff Natural Park but an area known for its own spectacular beauty, Lake Louise sits in a hanging valley, about 150 metres above the Bow River Valley. The incredible landscapes formed by Lake Louise, the mountains and glaciers have won Lake Louise accolades worldwide.

The Stoney Natives believed thunder rose from the emerald depths of Lake Louise, their "Lake of Little Fishes". But it's more likely that the vast glaciers clinging to the mountains' steep slopes sent thunderous sounds reverberating through the valley as great chunks of ice crashed down.

In 1882, Tom Wilson, the first white man to see Lake Louise, aptly named it Emerald Lake. When Wilson returned later, the lake had changed from green to blue, so he rechristened it Lake Louise for the daughter of his travelling companion.

The lake really does change colour with the seasons. In the summer, the silt, or cloudy rock flour increases as the ice melts and the silt disperses and reflects the green portion of the light spectrum. When the silt settles more quickly through the fall and spring, the water becomes a rich, deep blue.

Officially Lake Louise since 1884, Queen Victoria's fourth daughter, Princess Louise Caroline Alberta is more often credited with the lake's name than the daughter of Wilson's travelling companion. The province of Alberta is also named for Princess Louise and the mountain and glacier above the lake have Queen Victoria as their namesake.

Initially, Tom Wilson approved of the new name. "There are hundreds of Emerald Lakes, but there is but one Lake Louise." However, forty years after he first saw the lake, Wilson wrote in a letter, "The name was changed in 1884 locally to Louise (not Princess Louise)... What did Princess Louise ever do for Canada to have her name on the most beautiful spot in Canada...?"

In 1882, only Wilson and his Stoney Native guide, Edwin Hunter, saw Lake Louise. In 1893, just 50 visitors came, compared to 50,000 in 1912. Today more than 500,000 skiers visit the area each winter and there are at least that many summer tourists.

Even back in 1914, hikers and historians treasured the memory of Lake Louise "sans chalets and tourists", and Willoughby Astley, who managed the first "commodious" chalet from 1890 to 1894, called the building he saw in 1929, a "huge monstrosity".

Skiing, ice-sailing and skating are all popular sports that bring visitors flocking to the small town of Lake Louise. Two Olympic-class ski runs constructed in the 1960s added professional skiing status to the area and immediately enhanced its popularity.

And so it can be argued that the shores look better thanks to civilization. Chateau Lake Louise now sits on a shoreline that was once unattractive and worse, a swampy breeding ground for ravenous mosquitoes.

From Chateau Lake Louise, the scene changes according to the season, the weather and the time of day. The subtlety of a sunrise, the depth that comes as dusk falls and the visions created with mist and storm clouds all offer a new vision of Lake Louise.

CHATEAU LAKE LOUISE
Above

In a shack bearing the misspelled sign "Sumit Hotel", traveller A.P. Coleman spent a night in a bunk bed at the end of the CPR track in May 1884. When Coleman returned in 1907, he found a "comfortable hotel", which was destroyed by fire in 1924. The following year the predecessor of today's lovely, elegant Chateau Lake Louise was built and now welcomes guests from around the world.

CARIBOU
Above

The woodland caribou is about the size of an elk, but is usually darker in colour. In the mountains, caribou migrate vertically, seeking the alpine meadows in the summer and descending to the protected subalpine forest when the snows fall.

ALPINE FLORA
Right

Brilliantly hued, but seemingly fragile, these alpine flowers are a sharp contrast to the ten great peaks. Only in the Rockies do nature's smallest creations blend in such harmony with her most powerful.

NIGHT SPLENDOUR
Above

The perfect nightscape - a full moon lights the mountains. Only nature's illumination can do justice to the power and magnitude of the Rockies' highest peaks and its lowest valleys.

CROWFOOT MOUNTAIN
Left

Reflections of Crowfoot Mountain, to the west, are cast in Bow Lake. Crowfoot Glacier sits at the south end of the lake and Bow Glacier on the north-western side.

NOYES CREEK
Above

An impressive panorama of rock towers and pinnacles soars above Noyes Creek while misty morning steps softly into the meandering waterways of the Rockies and another magnificent day is born.

PEYTO LAKE
Left

Eccentric and legendary guide, Bill Peyto camped in splendid solitude on Peyto Lake's quiet shores in the Mistaya Valley. But even a century ago, he dubbed it "too crowded".

THE BOBCAT
Above

The bobcat, bay lynx or wild-
cat, is a close relative of the lynx and has long legs with large
paws and tufted ears. The bobcat is a nocturnal, solitary cat
that is at home in forests and deserts. It weighs seven to 15 kg.
(15 to 33 lbs.).

MOUNT FAIRVIEW
Left

The appealing summit view
gave Mount Fairview its name. It has also been known as Goat
Peak, since an exasperated Stoney Indian guide told two young
men from Yale, "You no see goat. You no got eyes," when they
couldn't spot the goats he'd shown them without the aid of
binoculars.

LAKE LOUISE
Above

The splendour and serenity
that is Lake Louise. As beautiful in the winter as it is enjoyable
in the summer, the Chateau and Lake Louise welcome
visitors year round.

MORAINE LAKE
Right

Moraine is a lake of many
moods. Minor shifts in weather and light change the colour
of the lake and the atmosphere of the valley. The close prox-
imity of the glowering mountain sentinels give this scene a
fierce ruggedness.

ASPEN
Above

The deciduous, fast-growing, moisture-loving aspen is a member of the poplar family. Its yellow-golden hues contrast beautifully against the steel grey mountains and emerald green lakes.

LUPINS
Right

These lupins are actually a member of the bean family, although its name is derived from "lupinus", the Latin word for wolf. People used to believe the lupin robbed the land of its minerals.

BIGHORN RAMS
Above

Butting bighorn rams fight head first every autumn and the winner takes the herd. Hear the resounding crack of this age-old contest echo through the mountains from year to year.

BOW LAKE
Left

A good place to cast for trout and spot moose, Bow Lake has the great ice-fields as a truly memorable backdrop.

WOLVES
Above

Wolves most usually travel in family units and it's believed they mate for life. A family group comprises the parents, the cubs from one or two litters, plus the occasional "aunt" or "uncle".

CROWFOOT GLACIER
Right

Crowfoot Glacier in all its majesty reflects the immensity and power of nature in full glory. The Rockies is an extravaganza of natural wonders like the mighty glaciers.

BLACK BEAR
Above

About 90 per cent of the black bear's diet is vegetarian, mixing roots, tubers and berries, according to the seasons. Just one per cent of their nourishment comes from fresh meat (animals they've caught and killed themselves).

AMERICAN KESTREL
Left

The American kestrel is a small bird of prey that hovers while hunting for large insects, birds and small mammals. In North America, it's commonly called the sparrow hawk.

PIKA
Above

The pika is a small, essentially tailless, rabbit-like mammal, approximately 15 to 30 cm. (four to 12 in.) long. Pikas harvest vegetation and dry it in the sun, then store it under rocks and in other protected places to eat during the winter.

CONSOLATION LAKE
Right

Consolation Lake is one of the prettiest subalpine lakes and one of the easiest to reach via a wide, gentle trail from Moraine Lake. Many of the lakes in the parks' back country require hours of uphill slogging.

Jasper National Park

MALIGNE LAKE
Above

Picture-perfect Maligne Lake got its ominous name from the treacherous currents that lurk where it joins the Athabasca River. It was originally dubbed "Sore-Foot Lake" by a weary railway surveyor in 1875.

MOUNT EDITH CAVELL
Left

Mount Edith Cavell shines brightly on sunny days, but also has its sombre moments, often hiding behind clouds. In October 1917, its namesake the British nurse Edith Cavell, was executed for helping allied soldiers escape occupied Belgium during World War I.

JASPER NATIONAL PARK

The Government proclaimed the Jasper area a national park in 1907, before the railway companies could despoil the wilderness. They hadn't forgotten the heated, ferocious arguments surrounding the ownership of Banff's hot springs and the ensuing damage done to forests, waterways and wildlife.

The town of "Fitzhugh" in 1911, became Jasper two years later, and even today, many buildings are of wood and stone, harmonizing with the surrounding forests and mountains. Not that long ago, Jasper townsite's population was easily two-thirds people and one-third bears. It was a rare trip to Jasper's downtown that didn't offer at least one bear sighting. But, there were few confrontations, precisely because the two species happily ignored one another, adopting a live-and-let-live attitude.

Generally, bears don't even like meeting people and will do whatever they can to avoid an encounter. As long as they can hear you coming, you won't need to worry about bears. It can be hard to tell the difference between a black bear and a grizzly, because the colour of both grizzlies and black bears runs the gamut of shades of light brown and tan to darker brown and black. As a result, colour is a less than reliable identifying characteristic. The grizzly's most recognizable feature is the prominent hump over the shoulders and a concave face from forehead to nose. Hopefully, you won't be close enough to note the grizzly's long curved claws. Those six-inch claws are ideal for digging up the grizzly's favourite roots and tubers. The black bear's claws are smaller and less visible. It has a straighter profile and no hump. Confusion reigns most often when the young grizzly is about the size of a large black bear.

Bears are omnivorous, but are primarily vegetarian. About 90 per cent of their diet is vegetarian, mixing roots, tubers and berries, according to the seasons, while nine per cent is carrion. Just one per cent is fresh meat from animals they've caught and killed themselves.

But bears aside, Jasper National Park is the largest National Park in the Canadian Rockies and is one of Canada's most magnificent natural museums.

Jasper is host to some of nature's most creative works of art. The monumental Columbia Icefield, for example, is the most extensive of the Rocky Mountain icefields. The area is a terrain of glacial ice that enveloped the northern regions of North America approximately 10,000 years ago. The icefield covers about 325 sq. km. (125 sq. miles) and is up to 385 metres (1,260 ft.) deep in some spots.

Carved and etched into the rock by the Maligne River is the awesome Maligne Canyon, with self-guiding trails and picturesque foot bridges that provide access to magnificent views. The highest of the Rockies' peaks stands tall and forbidding here. Mount Robson, also known as the Mountain of the Spiral Road, is an unforgettable sight at 3,954 metres. And mystical, some may even say magical, is Medicine Lake. Its waters rise and fall creating an enchanting lake in the summer months, but leaving little more than muddied clay flats in the fall.

Remarkable, mysterious and wild, Jasper, a mountain ecosystem that is nature-rich and beautiful.

GRANITE SPLENDOUR
Above

A harshly beautiful rock face in Jasper National Park. Composed of Precambrian, Paleozoic and Mesozoic sedimentary rock and lava flows, these granite natural wonders were formed over centuries by glacial erosion. Foreboding, forbidding and fearless...these magnificent mountains are awe-inspiring caught in a timeless world of beauty.

ATHABASCA GLACIER
Above

The most extensive Rocky Mountain icefield, the monumental Columbia Icefield, at the southern end of Jasper Park, covers about 325 sq. km. (125 sq. mi.) and is up to 385 metres (1,260 ft.) deep in some spots. About 100 years ago, the Athabasca Glacier covered the area the road now owns, but in 1873, the sun won the yearly battle, driving the glacier's "toe" back nearly two kilometres.

MOUNT ROBSON
Above

The icy crown of forbidding Mount Robson, also the Mountain of the Spiral Road, is an unforgettable sight, at 3,954 m., the highest of the Canadian Rockies.

ATHABASCA FALLS
Right

The Athabasca Falls come tumbling down. Thundering down its towering canyon, the Fall's majesty, power and strength are captured in its roar.

TIGER LILY
Above

The tiger lily's native home is the Far East, but this hardy lily grows well away from the soils of China and Japan.

PYRAMID MOUNTAIN
Left

Located less than 4 km. northwest of the town of Jasper, Pyramid Mountain resembles an ancient Egyptian monument built in honour of the gods.

MALIGNE LAKE
Above

Maligne Lake is the deepest
and largest lake in Jasper and one of the most popular areas for
fishing, hiking, or just simply getting back to Mother Nature.

TANGLE FALLS
Right

The beautiful falls that tumble
circuitously down the Tangle Ridge, were dubbed Tangle Falls
by a group of hikers that had trouble bushwhacking a direct
path. Today's path is maintained.

CHANGING SEASONS
Above

As autumn comes to the mountains, the meadows put on a real show. The Rockies incredible beauty is particularly highlighted during the change of seasons. Every moment of the year opens up new vistas, new experiences and more unparalleled beauty.

DANCE OF LIGHT
Right

Winter touches this scene with shafts of moonlight, snow and ice. Like a magical fairyland where dreams of unspoiled splendour are a reality.

RUFFLED GROUSE
Above

The ruffled grouse is coloured in wood-browns and greys. It has broad, soft, black feathers that form ruffs at the sides of the neck and a fan-shaped tail that whirs in flight.

MEDICINE LAKE
Left

Medicine Lake's waters rise and fall, swirling through distant subterranean tunnels, creating an enchanting summer lake in the warmer months, but leaving little more than muddied clay flats come fall.

SASKATCHEWAN GLACIER
Above

The Saskatchewan Glacier with an area of 23 sq. mi. (60 sq. km.) is the largest on the Columbia Icefield. Ice depths in this glacier have been measured to 1,450 ft. (442 m.). A large underground river system drains beneath the Columbia Icefield.

SUNWAPTA RIVER
Right

Split apart by a small rocky island, the Sunwapta River is reunited by a spectacular plunge at the Sunwapta Falls. The river is a gleaming silvered braid, spread across the valley floor in interlacing channels by sand and gravel.

Yoho National Park

EMERALD LAKE
Above

This gem of a lake, became so called when Lake Louise, nee Emerald, was renamed in 1884. This incredibly picturesque lake lies calmly at the foot of the Presidential Range in Yoho National Park.

TAKAKKAW FALLS
Left

Four local climbers successfully scaled the frozen Takakkaw Falls, one of Canada's highest waterfalls, more than two decades ago.

YOHO NATIONAL PARK

Yoho is the Cree word to express wonder or awe and with its rockwalls and waterfalls a most fitting name for this British Columbia park. With waterfalls, lakes and relatively speedy access to the upper subalpine and alpine ecoregions, hiking the Yoho Valley gives visitors a real taste of the Rockies' many facets and diverse ecosystems.

Yoho is the second smallest of the Canadian Rocky Mountain parks, encompassing 1,313 sq. km., with Banff to the east and Kootenay to the south.

1882 was an incredible year for Canadian Pacific Railway surveyor, Tom Wilson. First he discovered Lake Louise, then crossed Bow and Howse Passes, found ore on the slopes of Mount Stephen and discovered Yoho's jewel in the rough, Emerald Lake. This gem of a lake is so named because of its remarkable colour, the result of suspended rock-flour particles.

Yoho National Park's geological findings are diligently protected by the Park's guardians. The Burgess Shale, a site containing marine fossils of over 100 species that existed nearly 50 million years ago, was discovered by an American geologist in the early 1900s. In an effort to protect the delicate natural balance, bus tours into the Lake O'Hara area are limited. And to protect the grizzly bear populations, certain trails are closed off to the public from May to November each year.

The mountain experience can be more intimate in Yoho, where the Trans-Canada cuts under stunning peaks and shining waterfalls can be seen through the spring and summer.

Many visit Yoho for the Burgess Shale fossils, but the park also contains the most notorious length of railway track in Canada. The Spiral Tunnels were built to solve the problem of the sharp gradient up to Kicking Horse Pass.

The Yoho Valley, beyond Takakkaw Falls and Lake O'Hara, is great for hiking, while much of the park is serviced by the small town of Field.

Natural beauty that transfixes a visitor is all too common in the Rocky Mountain Parks, but in Yoho is especially stunning - Takakkaw Falls plunging 254 metres into the Yoho River below it, wears a rainbow halo as if it were more part of heaven than earth.

Yoho's spectacular scenery and over 400 km of hiking trails, offer visitors a look at nature that environmentalists work very hard to protect. In 1984 the park was declared a World Heritage site by UNESCO so that future generations may also appreciate the magnificence of nature untouched by the human hand.

THE BEAVER
Above

The beaver, as recognizable a symbol of Canada as the maple leaf, can weigh up to 60 lbs. (27 kg.) Beavers live in colonies, with one or more family groups per lodge. They slap the water with their broad, flat paddle-shaped tails to warn other beavers of danger.

LAKE McARTHUR
Right

Lake McArthur captured forever on a lovely mountain day. To preserve the grizzly bear populations in the area, the park closes off parts of the McArthur Pass to tourists from May to November annually.

MOUNT STEPHEN
Above

Though the Parks' natural resources were once plundered and abused by get-rich-quick explorers, today the delicate geological balance of nature is carefully protected. One such treasure is in the shales of Mount Stephen, about mid-mountain, where fossils were discovered in 1877 and the Stephen Fossil Bed and its trilobites became world-famous.

MOUNT HERBERT
Above

In the Rockies, the impact of climate and elevation on the soil is evident in the types of vegetation that grow in the montane, subalpine and alpine zones of the ranges. The great turreted peak of Mount Herbert watches over natural wonder Opabin Plateau, a flat-floored, lushly vegetated valley with undulating meadows, scattered stands of Lyall's larch and fir-edged reflecting ponds.

NATURAL BRIDGE
Above

Originally a waterfall, over time the constant surge of water caused the rocks to erode and form a new course of crevices through which the new river now flows.

TWIN PEAKS OF MOUNT GOODSIR
Right

A little shy, a tad bashful, the Twin Peaks of Mount Goodsir are the highest mountains in Yoho at 3,562 m (11,686 ft.), but are virtually hidden from anyone but the hardiest hikers and mountaineers.

Kananaskis Country

THREE SISTERS
Above

There's no sibling rivalry here as the Three Sisters reach toward the skies. The three peaks are not dissimilar in height with the tallest peak rising majestically at a little over 2 900 m (9,600 ft.).

MOUNT KIDD
Left

The castellate-type Mount Kidd boasts an old fire lookout on its grassy slope and was named for John Alfred Kidd, a store manager, who lived nearby in the tiny town of Morley.

KANANASKIS COUNTRY

Kananaskis was a native commemorated in local legend and the word has two meanings, "man with tomahawk in head" and "meeting of the waters". The Kananaskis River is a principal tributary of the Bow River and the two rivers merge near Bow Valley Provincial Park.

A multi-use area, incorporating three provincial parks, Peter Lougheed, Bow Valley and Bragg Creek, with natural areas, forest reserves, grazing lands, mining and petroleum leaseholds, there are over 3,000 auto-accessible campsites in some 20 campgrounds.

In 1988, Calgary hosted the Olympic Games and Canmore in Kananaskis was the site chosen for the nordic events. It was an interesting choice because the town is in a rain shadow with winter Chinook winds that frequent this part of the Bow Valley, raising temperatures and keeping snow cover to a minimum.

Canmore Nordic Centre hosted the nordic ski events and features 56 km. of cross-country ski trails that are used for hiking, mountain biking and interpretive walks in the summer.

The alpine or downhill skiing events are always a real highlight at Olympic Winter Games and back in 1988, the world focused on Nakiska at Mount Allan, the site of all alpine events. The entire Nakiska facility was built specifically for the Olympics and because the Chinook winds common to this area can cause air temperatures to rise by more than 20°C, Nakiska has extensive snow-making capabilities. Chinook is an Indian word that means "snow-eater".

The 1988 Winter Olympics are also fondly remembered for the appearance of the Jamaican Bobsled team, who inspired the Disney movie Cool Runnings starring Canada's own, the late great John Candy.

Kananaskis Country is doubly blessed with magnificent scenery and Kananaskis Village, a world-class destination resort with three fully-appointed resort hotels, as well as complete indoor and outdoor recreation facilities.

Lunar nightscapes, craggy towering peaks, wild-eyed flora... where else can man test his skills against nature's might, yet leave it unspoiled and intact.

LAKE CHESTER
Above

The flanks of Mount Chester ease into the southeast edge of Lake Chester and the outlet stream points to the distant peaks of the northern Spray Range. With urban dwellers' renewed interest in the endangered environment, protection of jewels like this sparkling lake amidst wildflower meadows and craggy peaks is now paramount.

MOUNT LORETTE
Above

Unlike most natural parks and sanctuaries of wildlife, the beloved Rocky Mountain peaks have taken on personas not always of their own. Many of these mountains have generals and battleships as their namesakes, but Mount Lorette was named by an explorer after a mountain range in France. Apparently, the mountaineer had spent a great deal of time climbing in France.

MOUNT LOUGHEED
Above

In the 1800s, Mount Lougheed was known as Wind Mountain because clouds gathered and curled around it, but it was rechristened in 1928 for the Honourable Sir James Lougheed (1854 - 1925).

CANADA LYNX
Left

A good swimmer and climber, the Canada lynx depends heavily on snowshoe rabbits for food. As a result, its population decreases and increases every nine or 10 years, following the cycles of its prey.

WATERTON LAKES NATIONAL PARK

PRINCE OF WALES HOTEL
Above

Poised on a hill, overlooking Upper Waterton, Bosporus and Middle Waterton Lakes, the seven-storey Prince of Wales Hotel made its debut in 1927.

WATERTON PEAKS
Left

Waterton's peaks are multi-coloured, tinted in delicately-hued red, green, brown, violet and tan shades, unlike the greys that dominate the mountain slopes to the north.

WATERTON LAKES NATIONAL PARK

If the Canadian Rockies have a backwater, it's Waterton Lakes tucked away in a quiet corner of southern Alberta. And those who come here have made a special trip because you don't end up in Waterton Lakes on your way to major attractions.

But, for a national park, these are good things - Waterton Park still has places where no human has ever set foot and other settings show no trace of human contact.

Crystal-clear alpine brooks and shining lakes, even the ageless mountain rocks seem entirely untouched.

Most of the year, the town of Waterton Park is a quiet place. In the winter, it resembles the timeless villages that grace glass paperweights where snow falls as they're up-ended.

Yet every short summer, this sleepy town awakens as shutters are lifted from cottage windows, shops and homes get a fresh coat of paint and Waterton Lakes becomes a bustling little resort town.

Many cottages have been in the family for two or three generations and Southern Albertans have a deep affection for this place and have great pride in its beauty.

Confirmed eccentric, explorer and naturalist Charles Waterton never saw the lakes, but he would have loved the great concentration of biological diversity that sees 25 different types of habitat in just 525 sq. km (203 sq. mi).

Theodore Roosevelt once said Waterton was the first field naturalist to ever write of "the magic and interest, the terror and beauty of the far-off wilds".

But Waterton's development, like other Rocky Mountain parks, was also fraught with difficulty at the beginning . After three years of drought, farmers were suffering and there was talk of putting a dam on the international waters between Upper and Middle Waterton Lakes. Back then, in 1919, that would have produced enough water to irrigate 75,000 acres of parched farmland. But American authorities wouldn't give their permission and worried park residents breathed a sigh of relief. A dam was later built east of the park on the Waterton River.

Construction on the Prince of Wales Hotel began in the winter of 1926 and was immediately struck by setbacks. Gusting Chinook winds blew the framework off centre and the design had to be changed. But over trials and tribulations and overlooking Upper Waterton Lake, the Bosporus and Middle Waterton Lakes, the seven-storey hotel made its debut in 1926 and remains today the picture-perfect retreat.

The scenery demands a certain respect, commands a definite reverence as the sweeping prairies roll golden against the rugged, reaching mountains. Waterton's peaks are multi-coloured, tinted in delicate hues of reds, greens and violet. Dramatic transitions and a bold study in nature's own contrasts... Waterton Lakes, where balsamroot and prairie crocus bloom and kestrels soar, while bear grass and mountain gentian cover alpine meadows and eagles ride the summer thermals, hovering for endless airborne moments.

RED ROCK CANYON
Above

Like a hand-painted tapestry, the Red Rock Canyon takes its name from the brightly coloured red-shale layers - a centuries-old metamorphosis that has created this incredible spectacle.

CROCUS
Right

The crocus flowers in the early spring or fall, but the blossoms close at night and when the weather is dull. The alpine species is the chief ancestor of the common garden crocus.

CAMERON LAKE
above

Well into summer, snow lingers on Mount Custer just inside the state of Montana, helping to feed Cameron Lake and keep it icy cold. This is a land of soaring mountain peaks, valleys sculptured over centuries by glacial erosions and alpine meadows dotted with brightly coloured wildflowers reaching toward the sky.

WATERTON
Above

Waterton has some of the oldest exposed bedrock in the Canadian Rockies. Erosions caused by extreme climate conditions constantly eat away at the rock faces, while melting glaciers nurture an abundance of lakes, streams, waterfalls and rare plant life that make this area one of the most diversely beautiful parklands in the Rockies.

ROCKY MOUNTAIN HIGHS
above

The Rocky Mountains were so named by the first travellers to experience the magnificence of these granite wonders as they towered towards the skies. "A small peak as a rule is the best view-point, because there is still something left to look up to..." J.M. Thorington, mountaineer.